W9-CFB-426

LITERARY LOVE

Skyhorse Publishing books may be purchased in bulk at special discounts for sales promotion, corporate gifts, fund-raising, or educational purposes. Special editions can also be created to specifications. For details, contact the Special Sales Department, Skyhorse Publishing, 307 West 36th Street, 11th Floor, New York, NY 10018 or info@skyhorsepublishing.com.

Skyhorse® and Skyhorse Publishing® are registered trademarks of Skyhorse Publishing, Inc.®, a Delaware corporation.

Visit our website at www.skyhorsepublishing.com.

10 9 8 7 6 5 4 3 2 1

Library of Congress Cataloging-in-Publication Data is available on file.

ISBN: 978-1-62636-575-9

Printed in China

LITERARY LOVE

Great Writers on Love and Romance

Isobel Carlson

A Herman Graf Book
Skyhorse Publishing

Dearest, – I wish I had the gift of making rhymes, for methinks there is poetry in my head and heart since I have been in love with you. You are a poem. You are a sort of sweet, simple, gay, pathetic ballad, which Nature is singing, sometimes with tears, sometimes with smiles, and sometimes intermingled smiles and tears.

Nathaniel Hawthorne to Sophie Hawthorne, 1839

How my heart beats when by accident I touch her finger, or my feet meet hers under the table! I draw back as if from a furnace; but a secret force impels me forward again, and my senses become disordered. Her innocent, unconscious heart never knows what agony these little familiarities inflict upon me. Sometimes when we are talking she lays her hand upon mine, and in the eagerness of conversation comes closer to me, and her balmy breath reaches my lips,—when I feel as if lightning had struck me, and that I could sink into the earth...

She is to me a sacred being. All passion is still in her presence: I cannot express my sensations when I am near her. I feel as if my soul beat in every nerve of my body. There is a melody which she plays on the piano with angelic skill,—so simple is it, and yet so spiritual! It is her favourite air; and, when she plays the first note, all pain, care, and sorrow disappear from me in a moment.

I believe every word that is said of the magic of ancient music. How her simple song enchants me!

Johann Wolfgang von Goethe,
The Sorrows of Young Werther

Desire

Where true Love burns Desire is Love's pure flame;
It is the reflex of our earthly frame,
That takes its meaning from the nobler part,
And but translates the language of the heart.

Samuel Taylor Coleridge

Love is that condition
in which the happiness
of another person is
essential to your own.

*Robert A. Heinlein, Stranger
in a Strange Land*

Believe Me, If All Those Endearing Young Charms

Believe me, if all those endearing young charms,
Which I gaze on so fondly today,
Were to change by tomorrow, and fleet in my arms,
Like fairy gifts fading away,
Thou wouldst still be adored, as this
moment thou art,
Let thy loveliness fade as it will,
And around the dear ruin each wish of my heart
Would entwine itself verdantly still.

It is not while beauty and youth are thine own,
And thy cheeks unprofaned by a tear
That the fervor and faith of a soul can be known,
To which time will but make thee more dear;
No, the heart that has truly loved never forgets,
But as truly loves on to the close,
As the sunflower turns on her god, when he sets,
The same look which she turned when he rose.

Thomas Moore

Come, O Come

Come, O come, my life's delight,
Let me not in languor pine!
Love loves no delay; thy sight,
The more enjoyed, the more divine:
O come, and take from me
The pain of being deprived of thee!

Thou all sweetness dost enclose,
Like a little world of bliss.
Beauty guards thy looks: the rose
In them pure and eternal is.
Come, then, and make thy flight
As swift to me, as heavenly light.

Thomas Campion

Jo never, *never* would learn to be proper, for when he said that as they stood upon the steps, she just put both hands into his, whispering *tenderly*, 'Not empty now,' and stooping down, kissed her Friedrich under the umbrella. It was dreadful, but she would have done it if the flock of draggle-tailed sparrows on the hedge had been human beings, for she was very far gone indeed, and quite regardless of everything but her own *happiness.* Though it came in such a very simple guise, that was the crowning moment of both their lives, when, turning from the night and storm and loneliness to the household light and warmth and peace waiting to receive them, with a glad *'Welcome home!'* Jo led her lover in, and shut the door.

Louisa May Alcott, Little Women

Beauty

I have seen dawn and sunset on moors
and windy hills
Coming in solemn beauty like slow
old tunes of Spain:
I have seen the lady April bringing in the daffodils,
Bringing the springing grass and the
soft warm April rain.

I have heard the song of the blossoms and
the old chant of the sea,
And seen strange lands from under the arched
white sails of ships;
But the loveliest things of beauty God
ever has showed to me
Are her voice, and her hair, and eyes,
and the dear red curve of her lips.

John Masefield

He first saw the old man; and then Christine entered, carrying the tea-tray. She flushed at the sight of Raoul, who went up to her and kissed her. She asked him a few questions, performed her duties as hostess prettily, took up the tray again and left the room. Then she ran into the garden and took refuge on a bench, a prey to feelings that stirred her young heart for the first time. Raoul followed her and they talked till the evening, very shyly. They were quite changed, cautious as two diplomatists, and told each other things that had nothing to do with their budding sentiments. When they took leave of each other by the roadside, Raoul, pressing a kiss on Christine's trembling hand, said:

'Mademoiselle, I shall never forget you!'

Gaston Leroux, The Phantom of the Opera

It was love at first sight,
at last sight, at ever
and ever sight.

Vladimir Nabokov, Lolita

A Letter To Her Husband

My head, my heart, mine eyes, my life, nay more,
My joy, my magazine of earthly store,
If two be one, as surely thou and I,
How stayest thou there, whilst I at Ipswich lie?
So many steps, head from the heart to sever,
If but a neck, soon should we be together...
I wish my Sun may never set, but burn
Within the Cancer of my glowing breast,
The welcome house of him my dearest guest.
Where ever, ever stay, and go not thence,
Till nature's sad decree shall call thee hence;
Flesh of thy flesh, bone of thy bone,
I here, thou there, yet both but one.

Anne Bradstreet

The Good-Morrow

I wonder, by my troth, what thou and I
Did, till we loved? Were we not weaned till then
But sucked on country pleasures, childishly?
Or snorted we in the seven sleepers' den?
'Twas so; but this, all pleasures fancies be.
If ever any beauty I did see,
Which I desired, and got, 'twas but a dream of thee.

And now good-morrow to our waking souls,
Which watch not one another out of fear;
For love all love of other sights controls,
And makes one little room an every where.
Let sea-discoverers to new worlds have gone,
Let maps to other, worlds on worlds have shown,
Let us possess one world; each hath one, and is one.

My face in thine eye, thine in mine appears,
And true plain hearts do in the faces rest;
Where can we find two better hemispheres,
Without sharp north, without declining west?
Whatever dies, was not mixed equally;
If our two loves be one, or, thou and I
Love so alike, that none do slacken, none can die.

John Donne

My dear Nora,

It has just struck me. I came in at half past eleven. Since then I have been sitting in an easy chair like a fool. I could do nothing. I hear nothing but your voice. I am like a fool hearing you call me 'Dear.' I offended two men today by leaving them coolly. I wanted to hear your voice, not theirs.

When I am with you I leave aside my contemptuous, suspicious nature. I wish I felt your head on my shoulder. I think I will go to bed.

I have been a half-hour writing this thing. Will you write something to me? I hope you will. How am I to sign myself? I won't sign anything at all, because I don't know what to sign myself.

James Joyce to Nora Barnacle, 1904

Who, being loved,
is poor?

Oscar Wilde

But now she triumphed, and the love so long pent up burst forth in full joyous bubblings. She tasted it without remorse, without anxiety, without trouble.

The day following passed with a new sweetness. They made vows to one another. She told him of her sorrows. Rodolphe interrupted her with kisses; and she looking at him through half-closed eyes, asked him to call her again by her name — to say that he loved her.

Gustave Flaubert, Madame Bovary

Wild Nights

Wild nights! Wild nights!
Were I with thee,
Wild nights should be
Our luxury!

Futile the winds
To a heart in port,
Done with the compass,
Done with the chart.

Rowing in Eden!
Ah! the sea!
Might I but moor
To-night in thee!

Emily Dickinson

Sonnet 116

Let me not to the marriage of true minds
Admit impediments. Love is not love
Which alters when it alteration finds,
Or bends with the remover to remove:
O no! it is an ever-fixed mark
That looks on tempests and is never shaken;
It is the star to every wandering bark,
Whose worth's unknown, although his
height be taken.
Love's not Time's fool, though rosy lips and cheeks
Within his bending sickle's compass come:
Love alters not with his brief hours and weeks,
But bears it out even to the edge of doom.
If this be error and upon me proved,
I never writ, nor no man ever loved.

William Shakespeare

Love knows not distance; it hath no continent; its eyes are for the stars, its feet for the swords; it continueth, though an army lay waste the pasture; it comforteth when there are no medicines; it hath the relish of manna; and by it do men live in the desert.

Gilbert Parker, Parables of a Province

Love does not consist
of gazing at each other,
but in looking outward
together in the same
direction.

Antoine de Saint-Exupéry

You fear, sometimes, I do not *love* you so much as you wish? My dear girl I love you ever and ever and without reserve. The more I have known you the more have I lov'd. In every way — even my jealousies have been *agonies* of love, in the hottest fit I ever had I would have died for you.

The last of your *kisses* was ever the sweetest; the last smile the brightest; the last movement the gracefullest. When you pass'd my window home yesterday, I was fill'd with as much *admiration* as if I had then seen you for the first time.

John Keats to Fanny Brawne, 1820

Again And Again,
However We Know The
Landscape Of Love

Again and again, however we know
the landscape of love
and the little churchyard there, with
its sorrowing names,
and the frighteningly silent abyss
into which the others
fall: again and again the two of us
walk out together
under the ancient trees, lie down
again and again
among the flowers, face to face
with the sky.

Rainer Maria Rilke

If I may so express it, I was steeped in Dora. I was not merely over head and ears in love with her, but I was saturated through and through. Enough love might have been wrung out of me, metaphorically speaking, to drown anybody in; and yet there would have remained enough within me, and all over me, to pervade my entire existence.

Charles Dickens, David Copperfield

Three Sunsets

He saw her once, and in the glance,
A moment's glance of meeting eyes,
His heart stood still in sudden trance:
He trembled with a sweet surprise —
All in the waning light she stood,
The star of perfect womanhood.

That summer eve his heart was light:
With lighter step he trod the ground:
And life was fairer in his sight,
And music was in every sound:
He blessed the world where there could be
So beautiful a thing as she.

Lewis Carroll

Love is composed of a
single soul inhabiting
two bodies.

Aristotle

The Exchange

We pledged our hearts, my love and I,
I in my arms the maiden clasping;
I could not tell the reason why,
But, O, I trembled like an aspen.

Her father's love she bade me gain;
I went, and shook like any reed!
I strove to act the main — in vain!
We had exchanged our hearts indeed.

Samuel Taylor Coleridge

O, how I hope that I am not estranging you even when I tell you that I love you wholly, that as long as I have known you, you have been to me 'half angel and half bird and all a wonder and a wild desire', that your influence alone can waken what is best in me.

Gordon Bottomley to Emily Burton, 1899

I have now been married ten years. I know what it is to live entirely for and with what I love best on earth. I hold myself supremely blest — blest beyond what language can express; because I am my husband's life as fully as he is mine. No woman was ever nearer to her mate than I am; ever more absolutely bone of his bone, and flesh of his flesh. I know no weariness of my Edward's society; he knows none of mine, any more than we each do of the pulsation of the heart that beats in our separate bosoms; consequently, we are ever together. To be together. To be together is for us to be at once as free as in solitude, as gay as in company. We talk, I believe, all day long; to talk to each other is but a more animated and an audible thinking. All my confidence is bestowed on him; all his confidence is devoted to me; we are precisely suited in character; perfect concord is the result.

Charlotte Brontë, Jane Eyre

The Oblation

Ask nothing more of me, sweet;
  All I can give you I give.
Heart of my heart, were it more,
More would be laid at your feet:
Love that should help you to live,
Song that should spur you to soar.

All things were nothing to give
Once to have sense of you more,
Touch you and taste of you sweet,
Think you and breathe you and live,
Swept of your wings as they soar,
Trodden by chance of your feet.

I that have love and no more
Give you but love of you, sweet:
He that hath more, let him give;
He that hath wings, let him soar;
  Mine is the heart at your feet
Here, that must love you to live.

Algernon Charles Swinburne

The moment we begin to seek love, love begins to seek us. And to save us.

Paulo Coelho, By the River Piedra I Sat Down and Wept

The Passionate Shepherd to His Love

Come live with me and be my love,
And we will all the pleasures prove,
That valleys, groves, hills and fields,
Woods or steepy mountains yields.

And we will sit upon the rocks,
Seeing the shepherds feed their flocks
By shallow rivers, to whose falls
Melodious birds sing madrigals.

And I will make thee beds of roses,
And a thousand fragrant posies,
A cap of flowers and a kirtle
Embroidered all with leaves of myrtle;

A gown made of the finest wool,
Which from our pretty lambs we pull;
Fair-lined slippers for the cold,
With buckles of the purest gold;

A belt of straw and ivy buds,
With coral clasps and amber studs;
And if these pleasures may thee move,
Come live with me and be my love.

The shepherd swains shall dance and sing
For thy delight each May morning;
If these delights thy mind may move,
Then live with me and be my love.

Christopher Marlowe

Pride had given way at last, obstinacy was gone: the will was powerless. He was but a man madly, blindly, *passionately* in love, and as soon as her light footsteps had died away within the house, he knelt down upon the terrace steps, and in the very madness of his love he *kissed* one by one the places where her small foot had trodden, and the stone balustrade there, where her tiny hand had *rested* last.

Baroness Orczy, *The Scarlet Pimpernel*

I cannot write my feelings in this large writing, begun on such a scale for the Review's sake; and just now — there is no denying it, and spite of all I have been incredulous about — it does seem that the fact *is* achieved and that I *do* love you, plainly, surely, more than ever, more than any day in my life before. It is your secret, the why, the how; the experience is mine. What are you doing to me? — in the heart's heart.

Rest — dearest — bless you — .

Robert Browning to Elizabeth Barrett Browning,
1846

Sonnet IX: Upon occasion of her walking in a garden

My lady's presence makes the roses red,
Because to see her lips they blush for shame;
The lily's leaves, for envy, pale became,
For her white hands in them this envy bred.
The marigold the leaves abroad doth spread,
Because the sun's and her power is the same.
The violet of purple colour came,
Dyed in the blood she made my heart to shed.
In brief, all flowers from her their virtue take;
From her sweet breath their sweet smells do proceed;
The living heat which her eyebeams do make
Warmeth the ground, and quickeneth the seed.
The rain, wherewith she watereth these flowers,
Falls from mine eyes, which she dissolves in showers.

Henry Constable

If I had a flower for every time I thought of you... I could walk through my garden forever.

Alfred, Lord Tennyson

What greater thing is there for two human souls, than to feel that they are joined for life – to strengthen each other in all labour, to rest on each other in all sorrow, to minister to each other in all pain, to be one with each other in silent unspeakable memories at the moment of the last parting?

George Eliot, Adam Bede

His heart beat faster and faster as Daisy's white face came up to his own. He knew that when he kissed this girl, and forever wed his unutterable visions to her perishable breath, his mind would never romp again like the mind of God. So he waited, listening for a moment longer to the tuning fork that had been struck upon a star. Then he kissed her. At his lips' touch she blossomed like a flower and the incarnation was complete.

F. Scott Fitzgerald, The Great Gatsby

My beloved angel,

I am nearly mad about you, as much as one can be mad: I cannot bring together two ideas that you do not interpose yourself between them.

I can no longer think of anything but you. In spite of myself, my imagination carries me to you. I grasp you, I kiss you, I caress you, a thousand of the most amorous caresses take possession of me.

As for my heart, there you will always be — very much so. I have a delicious sense of you there. But my God, what is to become of me, if you have deprived me of my reason? This is a monomania which, this morning, terrifies me.

I rise up every moment saying to myself, 'Come, I am going there!' Then I sit down again, moved by the sense of my obligations. There is a frightful conflict. This is not life. I have never before been like that. You have devoured everything.

I feel foolish and happy as soon as I think of you. I whirl round in a delicious dream in which in one instant I live a thousand years. What a horrible situation! Overcome with love, feeling love in every pore, living only for love, and seeing oneself consumed by griefs, and caught in a thousand spiders' threads.

O, my darling Eva, you did not know it. I picked up your card. It is there before me, and I talk to you as if you were there. I see you, as I did yesterday, beautiful, astonishingly beautiful.

Yesterday, during the whole evening, I said to myself 'she is mine!' Ah! The angels are not as happy in Paradise as I was yesterday!

Honoré de Balzac to Evelina Hanska, 1836

This hole in my heart is
in the shape of you and
no-one else can fit it.

Jeanette Winterson, Written on the Body

Perhaps, after all, romance did not come into one's life with pomp and blare, like a gay knight riding down; perhaps it crept to one's side like an old friend through quiet ways; perhaps it revealed itself in seeming prose, until some sudden shaft of illumination flung athwart its pages betrayed the rhythm and the music; perhaps... perhaps... love unfolded naturally out of a beautiful friendship, as a golden-hearted rose slipping from its green sheath.

L. M. Montgomery, Anne of Avonlea

I already love in you your *beauty*, but I am only beginning to love in you that which is eternal and ever precious — your heart, your *soul*. Beauty one could get to know and fall in love with in one hour and cease to *love* it as speedily; but the soul one must learn to know. Believe me, nothing on earth is given without labour, even love, the most beautiful and *natural* of feelings. But the more difficult the labour and hardship, the higher the reward.

Leo Tolstoy to Valeria Arsenev, 1856

She Walks in Beauty

She walks in beauty, like the night
Of cloudless climes and starry skies;
And all that's best of dark and bright
Meet in her aspect and her eyes:
Thus mellow'd to that tender light
Which heaven to gaudy day denies.

One shade the more, one ray the less,
Had half impaired the nameless grace
Which waves in every raven tress,
Or softly lightens o'er her face;
Where thoughts serenely sweet express
How pure, how dear their dwelling place.

And on that cheek, and o'er that brow,
So soft, so calm, yet eloquent,
The smiles that win, the tints that glow,
But tell of days in goodness spent,
A mind at peace with all below,
A heart whose love is innocent!

Lord Byron

When the palpitating creature was at last asleep in his arms he discovered that he was madly, was passionately, was overwhelmingly in love with her. It was a passion that had arisen like fire in dry corn. He could think of nothing else; he could live for nothing else.

Ford Madox Ford,
The Good Soldier: A Tale of Passion

When I saw her I was
in love with her.

Ernest Hemingway, A Farewell to Arms

My mistress and friend, I and my heart put ourselves in your hands, begging you to recommend us to your favour, and not to let absence lessen your affection to us. For it were a great pity to increase our pain, which absence alone does sufficiently, and more than I could ever have thought; bringing to my mind a point of astronomy, which is, That the farther the Moors are from us, the farther too is the sun, and yet his heat is the more scorching; so it is with our love, we are at a distance from one another, and yet it keeps its fervency, at least on my side. I hope the like on your part, assuring you that the uneasiness of absence is already too severe for me; and when I think of the continuance of that which I must of necessity suffer, it would seem intolerable to me, were it not for the firm hope I have of your unchangeable affection for me; and now, to put you sometimes in mind of it, and seeing I cannot be present in person with you, I send you the nearest thing to that possible, that is, my picture set in bracelets, with the whole device, which you know already, wishing myself in their place, when it shall please you.

This from the hand of
Your servant and friend H. Rex

Henry VIII to Anne Boleyn

Song: To Celia

Drink to me, only with thine eyes
And I will pledge with mine;
Or leave a kiss but in the cup,
And I'll not look for wine.
The thirst that from the soul doth rise
Doth ask a drink divine:
But might I of Jove's nectar sup
I would not change for thine.

I sent thee late a rosy wreath,
Not so much honouring thee
As giving it a hope that there
It could not withered be
But thou thereon didst only breathe
And sent'st it back to me:
Since, when it grows and smells, I swear,
Not of itself but thee.

Ben Jonson

The great tragedy of life
is not that men perish,
but that they cease
to love.

W. Somerset Maugham

'You pierce my soul. I am half agony, half hope. Tell me not that I am too late, that such precious feelings are gone for ever. I offer myself to you again with a heart even more your own than when you almost broke it, eight years and a half ago. Dare not say that man forgets sooner than woman, that his love has an earlier death. I have loved none but you.'

Jane Austen, Persuasion

No, nothing has the power to part me from you; our love is based upon virtue, and will last as long as our lives.

Adieu, there is nothing that I will not brave for your sake; you deserve much more than that.

Adieu, my dear heart!

Voltaire to Marquise Gabrielle

Love is no hot-house flower, but a *wild* plant, born of a wet night, born of an hour of sunshine; sprung from wild seed, blown along the road by a wild wind. A wild plant that, when it *blooms* by chance within the hedge of our gardens, we call a flower; and when it blooms outside we call a weed; but, *flower* or weed, whose *scent* and colour are always, wild!

John Galsworthy, *The Forsyte Saga*

To My Dear and Loving Husband

If ever two were one, then surely we.
If ever man were lov'd by wife, then thee;
If ever wife was happy in a man,
Compare with me ye women if you can.
I prize thy love more then whole Mines of gold,
Or all the riches that the East doth hold.
My love is such that Rivers cannot quench,
Nor ought but love from thee, give recompence.
Thy love is such I can no way repay,
The heavens reward thee manifold I pray.
Then while we live, in love let's so persever,
That when we live no more, we may live ever.

Anne Bradstreet

My dearest,

When two souls, which have sought each other for, however long in the throng, have finally found each other... a union, fiery and pure as they themselves are... begins on earth and continues forever in heaven.

This union is love, true love... a religion, which deifies the loved one, whose life comes from devotion and passion, and for which the greatest sacrifices are the sweetest delights.

This is the love which you inspire in me... Your soul is made to love with the purity and passion of angels; but perhaps it can only love another angel, in which case I must tremble with apprehension.

Yours forever.

Victor Hugo to Adèle Foucher, 1821

If a thing loves,
it is infinite.

William Blake

Miss Morstan and I stood together, and her hand was in mine. A wondrous subtle thing is love, for here were we two who had never seen each other before that day, between whom no word or even look of affection had ever passed, and yet now in an hour of trouble our hands instinctively sought for each other. I have marvelled at it since, but at the time it seemed the most natural thing that I should go out to her so, and, as she has often told me, there was in her also the instinct to turn to me for comfort and protection. So we stood hand in hand, like two children, and there was peace in our hearts for all the dark things that surrounded us.

Arthur Conan Doyle, The Sign of the Four

Air and Angels

Twice or thrice had I lov'd thee,
Before I knew thy face or name;
So in a voice, so in a shapeless flame
Angels affect us oft, and worshipp'd be;
Still when, to where thou wert, I came,
Some lovely glorious nothing I did see.
But since my soul, whose child love is,
Takes limbs of flesh, and else could nothing do,
More subtle than the parent is
Love must not be, but take a body too;
And therefore what thou wert, and who,
I bid Love ask, and now
That it assume thy body, I allow,
And fix itself in thy lip, eye, and brow.

Whilst thus to ballast love I thought,
And so more steadily to have gone,
With wares which would sink admiration,
I saw I had love's pinnace overfraught;

Ev'ry thy hair for love to work upon
Is much too much, some fitter must be sought;
For, nor in nothing, nor in things
Extreme, and scatt'ring bright, can love inhere;
Then, as an angel, face, and wings
Of air, not pure as it, yet pure, doth wear,
So thy love may be my love's sphere;
Just such disparity
As is 'twixt air and angels' purity,
'Twixt women's love, and men's, will ever be.

John Donne

Dear Anna:

Did I say that the human might be filed in categories? Well, and if I did, let me qualify -- not all humans. You elude me. I cannot place you, cannot grasp you. I may boast that of nine out of ten, under given circumstances, I can forecast their action; that of nine out of ten, by their word or action, I may feel the pulse of their hearts. But of the tenth I despair. It is beyond me. You are that tenth.

Were ever two souls, with dumb lips, more incongruously matched! We may feel in common — surely, we oftimes do — and when we do not feel in common, yet do we understand; and yet we have no common tongue. Spoken words do not come to us. We are unintelligible. God must laugh at the mummery...

Am I unintelligible now? I do not know. I imagine so. I cannot find the common tongue.

Jack London to Anna Strunsky, 1901

I have succeeded as
gloriously as anyone
who's ever lived: I've
loved another with all
my heart and soul.

Nicholas Sparks, The Notebook

He had never before seen a woman's *lips* and teeth which forced upon his mind with such persistent iteration the old Elizabethan simile of *roses* filled with snow. *Perfect,* he, as a lover, might have called them off-hand. But no — they were not perfect. And it was the touch of the imperfect upon the would-be perfect that gave the *sweetness,* because it was that which gave the humanity.

Thomas Hardy, Tess of the D'Urbervilles

My love for you tonight is so deep and tender that it seems to be outside myself as well. I am fast shut up like a little lake in the embrace of some big mountains. If you were to climb up the mountains you would see me down below, deep and shining — and quite fathomless, my dear. You might drop your heart into me and you'd never hear it touch bottom. I love you — I love you — Goodnight. Oh Bogey, what it is to love like this!

Katherine Mansfield to John Middleton Murray

My love for Linton is like the foliage in the woods: time will change it, I'm well aware, as winter changes the trees. My love for Heathcliff resembles the eternal rocks beneath: a source of little visible delight, but necessary. Nelly, I am Heathcliff! He's always, always in my mind: not as a pleasure, any more than I am always a pleasure to myself, but as my own being.

Emily Brontë, Wuthering Heights

Now Sleeps the Crimson Petal, Now the White

Now sleeps the crimson petal, now the white;
Nor waves the cypress in the palace walk;
Nor winks the gold fin in the porphyry font:
The fire-fly wakens; waken thou with me.

Now droops the milkwhite peacock like a ghost,
And like a ghost she glimmers on to me.

Now lies the Earth all Danaë to the stars,
And all thy heart lies open unto me.

Now slides the silent meteor on, and leaves
A shining furrow, as thy thoughts in me.

Now folds the lily all her sweetness up,
And slips into the bosom of the lake:
So fold thyself, my dearest, thou, and slip
Into my bosom and be lost in me.

Alfred, Lord Tennyson

Love is the ultimate
outlaw. It just won't
adhere to any rules.

Tom Robbins, Still Life with Woodpecker

'Fancied, or not fancied — I question not myself to know which — I choose to believe that I owe my very life to you — ay — smile, and think it an exaggeration if you will. I believe it, because it adds a value to that life to think — oh, Miss Hale!' continued he, lowering his voice to such a tender intensity of passion that she shivered and trembled before him, 'to think circumstance so wrought, that whenever I exult in existence henceforward, I may say to myself, "All this gladness in life, all honest pride in doing my work in the world, all this keen sense of being, I owe to her!" And it doubles the gladness, it makes the pride glow, it sharpens the sense of existence till I hardly know if it is pain or pleasure, to think that I owe it to one — nay, you must, you shall hear' — said he, stepping forwards with stern determination — 'to one whom I love, as I do not believe man ever loved woman before.' He held her hand tight in his. He panted as he listened for what should come.

Elizabeth Gaskell, North and South

What Little Things!

What little things are those
That hold our happiness!
A smile, a glance, a rose
Dropped from her hair or dress;
A word, a look, a touch,—
These are so much, so much.

An air we can't forget;
A sunset's gold that gleams;
A spray of mignonette,
Will fill the soul with dreams
More than all history says,
Or romance of old days.

For of the human heart,
Not brain, is memory;
These things it makes a part
Of its own entity;
The joys, the pains whereof
Are the very food of love.

Madison Cawein

When you fall in love, it is a temporary madness. It erupts like an earthquake.

Louis de Bernières,
Captain Corelli's Mandolin

If only I were a clever woman, I could describe to you my *gorgeous* bird, how you unite in yourself the beauties of form, plumage, and song!

I would tell you that you are the greatest *marvel* of all ages, and I should only be speaking the simple truth. But to put all this into suitable words, my *superb* one, I should require a voice far more harmonious than that which is bestowed upon my species —

I will not tell you to what degree you are dazzling and to the birds of *sweet* song who, as you know, are none the less beautiful and appreciative.

I *love* you, I love you. My Victor; I can not reiterate it too often; I can never express it as much as I feel it.

Juliette Drouet to Victor Hugo

'Then must you strive to be worthy of her love. Be brave and pure, fearless to the strong and humble to the weak; and so, whether this love prosper or no, you will have fitted yourself to be honoured by a maiden's love, which is, in sooth, the highest guerdon which a true knight can hope for.'

Arthur Conan Doyle, The White Company

'I should not have believed anyone who told me that I was capable of such love,' said Prince Andrew. 'It is not at all the same feeling that I knew in the past. The whole world is now for me divided into two halves: one half is she, and there all is joy, hope, light: the other half is everything where she is not, and there is all gloom and darkness...'

Leo Tolstoy, War and Peace

I am reduced to a thing that wants Virginia. I just miss you, in a quite simple desperate human way.

Vita Sackville-West to Virginia Woolf, 1926

Love

YES, Love has his changes, but be not too ready,
To number his faults or dishonour his sway;
Abuse him you may, as the billow unsteady,
But what are his changes? say, Moralist, say.
At first, I confess, full of whims and vagaries,
All wing and all fire, a wild boy and no more;
But pass a few years—then observe how he varies;
His freaks disappear, and his follies are o'er.
And who would now blame him? so alter'd a creature
More sweet is his smile, more contented his air;
More happy his mien, tho' more sober each feature,
And look at his form! see, no pinions are there.
We journey thro' life, and the hill now ascending,
New changes in life must too surely appear;
Inverted his torch, and on earth his eyes bending,
He moves a lone mourner, and follows a bier.

Then cold to the world, from its pleasures retiring,
He comes like a pilgrim to memory's shrine;
Anal whisp'ring new hopes, and, new visions inspiring,
The child is now chang'd to a seraph divine.

Joanna Baillie

It is my lady; O, it is my love!
O that she knew she were!
She speaks, yet she says nothing. What of that?
Her eye discourses; I will answer it.
I am too bold; 'tis not to me she speaks.
Two of the fairest stars in all the heaven,
Having some business, do entreat her eyes
To twinkle in their spheres till they return.
What if her eyes were there, they in her head?
The brightness of her cheek would shame those stars
As daylight doth a lamp; her eyes in heaven
Would through the airy region stream so bright
That birds would sing and think it were not night.
See how she leans her cheek upon her hand!
O that I were a glove upon that hand,
That I might touch that cheek!

*William Shakespeare, Romeo and Juliet,
Act 2, Scene 2*

Love is an
irresistible desire to be
irresistibly desired.

Robert Frost

You are my only love.

You have me completely in your power.

I know and feel that if I am to write anything fine and noble in the future I shall do so only by listening at the doors of your heart.

I would like to go through life side by side with you, telling you more and more until we grew to be one being together until the hour should come for us to die.

James Joyce to Nora Barnacle, 1909

A Red Red Rose

O my luve's like a red, red rose
That's newly sprung in June;
O my luve's like the melodie
That's sweetly play'd in tune.

As fair art thou, my bonnie lass,
So deep in luve am I;
And I will luve thee still, my dear,
Till a' the seas gang dry:

Till a' the seas gang dry, my dear,
And the rocks melt wi' the sun;
I will luve thee still, my dear,
While the sands o' life shall run.

And fare thee weel, my only Luve,
And fare thee weel, a while!
And I will come again, my luve,
Tho' it were ten thousand mile.

Robert Burns

Once for all; I knew to my *sorrow,* often and often, if not always, that I loved her against reason, against promise, against peace, against *hope,* against happiness, against all discouragement that could be. Once for all; I *loved* her none the less because I knew it, and it had no more influence in restraining me than if I had devoutly believed her to be human *perfection.*

Charles Dickens, Great Expectations

Eros

The sense of the world is short,
Long and various the report,
To love and be beloved;
Men and gods have not outlearned it,
And how oft soe'er they've turned it,
'Tis not to be improved.

Ralph Waldo Emerson

There is never a time
or place for true love.
It happens accidentally,
in a heartbeat...

Sarah Dessen, The Truth About Forever

My dearest Teresa, —

I have read this book in your garden; — my love, you were absent, or else I could not have read it. It is a favourite book of yours, and the writer was a friend of mine. You will not understand these English words, and others will not understand them, — which is the reason I have not scrawled them in Italian. But you will recognize the handwriting of him who passionately loves you, and you will divine that, over a book which was yours, he could only think of love. In that word, beautiful in all languages, but most so in yours — Amor mio — is comprised my existence here and hereafter. I feel I exist here, and I fear that I shall exist hereafter, — as to what purpose you will decide; my destiny rests with you, and you are a woman, seventeen years of age, and two out of a convent. I wish that you had stayed there, with all my heart, — or, at least, that I had never met you in your married state.

But all this is too late. I love you, and you love me, — at least, you say so, and act as if you did so, which last is a great consolation in all events. But I more than love you, and cannot cease to love you.

Think of me, sometimes, when the Alps and the ocean divide us, — but they never will, unless you wish it.

Lord Byron to the Countess Teresa Guiccioli, 1819

By every vessel he wrote; he wrote as he gave and as he loved, in full-handed, full-hearted plenitude. He wrote because he liked to write; he did not abridge, because he cared not to abridge. He sat down, he took pen and paper, because he loved Lucy and had much to say to her; because he was faithful and thoughtful; because he was tender and true. There was no sham and no cheat, and no hollow unreal in him... his letters were real food that nourished, living water that refreshed.

Charlotte Brontë, Villette

A Drinking Song

Wine comes in at the mouth
And love comes in at the eye;
That's all we shall know for truth
Before we grow old and die.
I lift the glass to my mouth,
I look at you, and I sigh.

W. B. Yeats

Because She Would Ask Me Why I Loved Her

If questioning would make us wise
No eyes would ever gaze in eyes;
If all our tale were told in speech
No mouths would wander each to each.

Were spirits free from mortal mesh
And love not bound in hearts of flesh
No aching breasts would yearn to meet
And find their ecstasy complete.

For who is there that lives and knows
The secret powers by which he grows?
Were knowledge all, what were our need
To thrill and faint and sweetly bleed?

Then seek not, sweet, the "If" and "Why"
I love you now until I die.
For I must love because I live
And life in me is what you give.

Christopher Brennan

You know you're
in love when you can't
fall asleep because
reality is finally better
than your dreams.

Dr. Seuss

Adam looked at her. It was so *sweet* to look at her eyes, which had now a self-forgetful questioning in them — for a moment he forgot that he wanted to say anything, or that it was *necessary* to tell her what he meant.

'Dinah,' he said suddenly, taking both her hands between his, 'I love you with my whole *heart and soul.* I love you next to God who made me.'

George Eliot, *Adam Bede*

I Have No Life But This

I have no life but this,
To lead it here;
Nor any death, but lest
Dispelled from there;

Nor tie to earths to come,
Nor action new,
Except through this extent,
The realm of you.

Emily Dickinson

'It has made me better loving you... it has made me wiser, and easier, and brighter. I used to want a great many things before, and to be angry that I did not have them. Theoretically, I was satisfied. I flattered myself that I had limited my wants. But I was subject to irritation; I used to have morbid sterile hateful fits of hunger, of desire. Now I really am satisfied, because I can't think of anything better.'

Henry James, The Portrait of a Lady

I am always conscious
of my nearness to you,
your presence never
leaves me.

*Johann Wolfgang von Goethe to
Charlotte von Stein, 1784*

Love looks not with the eyes, but with the mind.

William Shakespeare, A Midsummer Night's Dream, Act 1, Scene 1

The Sea Hath Its Pearls

The sea hath its pearls
The heaven hath its stars;
But my heart, my heart,
My heart hath its love.

Great are the sea, and the heaven;
Yet greater is my heart,
And fairer than pearls or stars
Flashes and beams my love.

Thou little, youthful maiden,
Come unto my great heart;
My heart, and the sea and the heaven
Are melting away with love!

Heinrich Heine

Love has no other desire but to fulfil itself.
But if you love and must needs have desires,
let these be your desires:
To melt and be like a running brook that sings
its melody to the night.
To know the pain of too much tenderness.
To be wounded by your own understanding of love;
And to bleed willingly and joyfully.
To wake at dawn with a winged heart and give
thanks for another day of loving;
To rest at the noon hour and meditate love's ecstasy;
To return home at eventide with gratitude;
And then to sleep with a prayer for the beloved in
your heart and a song of praise upon your lips.

Kahlil Gibran, The Prophet

I will cover you with love when next I see you, with caresses, with ecstasy. I want to gorge you with all the joys of the flesh, so that you faint and die. I want you to be amazed by me, and to confess to yourself that you had never even dreamed of such transports... When you are old, I want you to recall those few hours, I want your dry bones to quiver with joy when you think of them.

Gustave Flaubert to Louise Colet, 1846

Out of the depths of my happy heart wells a great tide of love and prayer for this priceless treasure that is confided to my life-long keeping.

You cannot see its intangible waves as they flow towards you, darling, but in these lines you will hear, as it were, the distant beating of the surf.

Mark Twain to Olivia Langdon, 1869

One is loved because
one is loved. No reason
is needed for loving.

Paulo Coelho, The Alchemist

She's a danger mortal,
All unsuspicious — full of charms unconscious,
Like a sweet perfumed rose — a snare of nature,
Within whose petals Cupid lurks in ambush!
He who has seen her smile has known perfection,
— Instilling into trifles grace's essence,
Divinity in every careless gesture;
Not Venus' self can mount her conch
blown sea-ward,
As she can step into her chaise à porteurs,
Nor Dian fleet across the woods spring-flowered,
Light as my Lady o'er the stones of Paris!

Edmond Rostand, Cyrano de Bergerac,
Act 1, Scene 5

Dear Madam,

The passion of love has need to be productive of much delight; as where it takes thorough possession of the man, it almost unfits him for anything else.

The lover who is certain of an equal return of affection, is surely the happiest of men; but he who is a prey to the horrors of anxiety and dreaded disappointment, is a being whose situation is by no means enviable.

Of this, my present experience gives me much proof. To me, amusement seems impertinent, and business intrusion, while you alone engross every faculty of my mind.

May I request you to drop me a line, to inform me when I may wait upon you?

For pity's sake, do; and let me have it soon.

In the meantime allow me, in all the artless sincerity of truth, to assure you that I truly am,

my dearest Madam,

your ardent lover, and devoted humble servant.

A love letter by Robert Burns to an unknown recipient

Sonnet 43

How do I love thee? Let me count the ways.
I love thee to the depth and breadth and height
My soul can reach, when feeling out of sight
For the ends of Being and ideal Grace.
I love thee to the level of everyday's
Most quiet need, by sun and candle-light.
I love thee freely, as men strive for Right;
I love thee purely, as they turn from Praise.
I love thee with the passion put to use
In my old griefs, and with my childhood's faith.
I love thee with a love I seemed to lose
With my lost saints, — I love thee with the breath,
Smiles, tears, of all my life! — and, if God choose,
I shall but love thee better after death.

Elizabeth Barrett Browning

Maggie said that love was the *flower* of life, and blossomed unexpectedly and without law, and must be plucked where it was found, and *enjoyed* for the brief hour of its duration.

To Ursula this was unsatisfactory... She believed that *love* was a way, a means, not an end in itself, as Maggie seemed to think. And always the way of love would be *found.* But whither did it lead?

D. H. Lawrence, The Rainbow

Every heart sings
a song, incomplete,
until another heart
whispers back...
At the touch of a
lover, everyone
becomes a poet.

Plato

I have not spent a day without loving you; I have not spent a night without embracing you; I have not so much as drunk a single cup of tea without cursing the pride and ambition which force me to remain separated from the moving spirit of my life.

In the midst of my duties, whether I am at the head of my army or inspecting the camps, my beloved Josephine stands alone in my heart, occupies my mind, fills my thoughts.

If I am moving away from you with the speed of the Rhone torrent, it is only that I may see you again more quickly.

If I rise to work in the middle of the night, it is because this may hasten by a matter of days the arrival of my sweet love.

Napoleon Bonaparte to
Joséphine de Beauharnais

She Comes Not When Noon is on the Roses

She comes not when Noon is on the roses –
Too bright is Day.
She comes not to the Soul till it reposes
From work and play.

But when Night is on the hills, and the great
Voices Roll in from Sea,
By starlight and by candlelight and dreamlight
She comes to me.

Herbert Trench

Jenny Kissed Me

Jenny kissed me when we met,
Jumping from the chair she sat in.
Time, you thief! who love to get
Sweets into your list, put that in.
Say I'm weary, say I'm sad;
Say that health and wealth have missed me;
Say I'm growing old, but add,
Jenny kissed me!

Leigh Hunt

To love is good, too: love being difficult. For one human being to love another: that is perhaps the most difficult of all our tasks, the ultimate, the last test and proof, the work for which all other work is but preparation... Love is a high inducement to the individual to ripen, to become something in himself, to become world for himself for another's sake, it is a great exacting claim upon him, something that chooses him out and calls him to vast things.

Rainer Maria Rilke, Letters to a Young Poet

I love. I have loved.
I will love.

Audrey Niffenegger,
The Time Traveler's Wife

Tell me whence
these uncanny
disturbances spring,
these inexpressible
foretastes of delight,
these divine tremors
of love.

Franz Liszt to Marie d'Agoult

'You anticipate what I would say, though you cannot know how earnestly I say it, how earnestly I feel it, without knowing my secret heart, and the hopes and fears and anxieties with which it has long been laden. Dear Doctor Manette, I love your daughter fondly, dearly, disinterestedly, devotedly. If ever there were love in the world, I love her.'

Charles Dickens, A Tale of Two Cities

Amoretti: Sonnet 64

Coming to kiss her lips (such grace I found),
Me seem'd I smelt a garden of sweet flow'rs
That dainty odours from them threw around,
For damsels fit to deck their lovers' bow'rs.
Her lips did smell like unto gilliflowers,
Her ruddy cheeks like unto roses red,
Her snowy brows like budded bellamoures,
Her lovely eyes like pinks but newly spread,
Her goodly bosom like a strawberry bed,
Her neck like to a bunch of cullambines,
Her breast like lilies ere their leaves be shed,
Her nipples like young blossom'd jessamines:
Such fragrant flow'rs do give most odourous smell,
But her sweet odour did them all excel.

Edmund Spenser

Directly she had gone out, swift, swift light steps sounded on the parquet, and his *bliss,* his life, himself – what was best in himself, what he had so long sought and *longed* for – was quickly, so quickly approaching him. She did not walk, but seemed, by some unseen force, to float to him. He saw nothing but her clear, truthful eyes, frightened by the same bliss of love that flooded his heart. Those eyes were shining nearer and nearer, blinding him with their light of love. She stopped still close to him, *touching* him. Her hands rose and dropped onto his shoulders.

She had done all she could – she had run up to him and given herself up entirely, shy and happy. He put his arms round her and pressed his *lips* to her mouth that sought his kiss.

Leo Tolstoy, *Anna Karenina*

Never close your lips
to those whom you
have already opened
your heart.

Charles Dickens,
Master Humphrey's Clock

We clung to each other with a rather silly desperation... we became inseparable, two halves creating the whole: yin and yang.

Amy Tan, The Joy Luck Club

'You love me then?' said he, fervently pressing my hand.

'Yes.'

Here I pause. My Diary, from which I have compiled these pages, goes but little further. I could go on for years, but I will content myself with adding, that I shall never forget that glorious summer evening, and always remember with delight that steep hill, and the edge of the precipice where we stood together, watching the splendid sunset mirrored in the restless world of waters at our feet — with hearts filled with gratitude to heaven, and happiness, and love — almost too full for speech.

Anne Brontë, Agnes Grey

Was this the face that launched a thousand ships
    And burnt the topless towers of Ilium?
Sweet Helen, make me immortal with a kiss.
Her lips suck forth my soul; see where it flies!—
    Come, Helen, come, give me my soul again.
Here will I dwell, for Heaven is in these lips,
    And all is dross that is not Helena.
    I will be Paris, and for love of thee,
Instead of Troy, shall Wittenberg be sack'd;
    And I will combat with weak Menelaus,
And wear thy colours on my plumed crest;
    Yea, I will wound Achilles in the heel,
    And then return to Helen for a kiss
    Oh, thou art fairer than the evening air
    Clad in the beauty of a thousand stars;
    Brighter art thou than flaming Jupiter
    When he appear'd to hapless Semele:
More lovely than the monarch of the sky
    In wanton Arethusa's azured arms:
And none but thou shalt be my paramour.

Christopher Marlowe, Doctor Faustus,
Act 5 Scene 1

... much abashed with joy, was I, when I saw my Lorna coming, purer than the morning dew, than the sun more bright and clear. That which made me love her so, that which lifted my heart to her, as the Spring wind lifts the clouds, was the gayness of her nature, and its inborn playfulness. And yet all this with maiden shame, a conscious dream of things unknown, and a sense of fate about them.

Down the valley still she came, not witting that I looked at her, having ceased (through my own misprison) to expect me yet awhile; or at least she told herself so. In the joy of awakened life and brightness of the morning, she had cast all care away, and seemed to float upon the sunrise, like a buoyant silver wave. Suddenly at sight of me, for I leaped forth at once, in fear of seeming to watch her unawares, the bloom upon her cheeks was deepened, and the radiance of her eyes; and she came to meet me gladly.

R. D. Blackmore, Lorna Doone

You have made a place
in my heart where I
thought there was no
room for anything else.

Robert Jordan, The Wheel of Time

First Love

I ne'er was struck before that hour
With love so sudden and so sweet;
Her face it bloomed like a sweet flower
And stole my heart away complete.
My face turned pale as deadly pale,
My legs refused to walk away,
And when she looked what could I ail?
My life and all seemed turned to clay.

And then my blood rushed to my face
And took my eyesight quite away;
The trees and bushes round the place
Seemed midnight at noonday.
I could not see a single thing,
Words from my eyes did start;
They spoke as chords do from the string
And blood burnt round my heart.

Are flowers the winter's choice?
Is love's bed always snow?
She seemed to hear my silent voice,
Not love's appeals to know.
I never saw so sweet a face
As that I stood before;
My heart has left its dwelling place
And can return no more.

John Clare

Never was *passion* so tender and so violent as that of Monsieur de Nemours; he walked under the willows, along a little brook which ran behind the house, where he lay concealed; he kept himself as much out of the way as possible, that he might not be seen by anybody; he abandoned himself to the transports of his *love,* and his heart was so full of *tenderness,* that he was forced to let fall some tears, but those tears were such as grief alone could not shed; they had a mixture of sweetness and *pleasure* in them which is to be found only in love.

Madame de La Fayette, *The Princess of Cleves*

That quiet mutual gaze of a trusting husband and wife is like the first moment of rest or refuge from a great weariness or a great danger – not to be interfered with by speech or action which would distract the sensations from the fresh enjoyment of repose.

George Eliot, Silas Marner

Love's Philosophy

The fountains mingle with the river
And the rivers with the ocean,
The winds of Heaven mix forever
With a sweet emotion;
Nothing in the world is single;
All things by a law divine
In one spirit meet and mingle.
Why not I with thine? –

See the mountains kiss high Heaven
And the waves clasp one another;
No sister-flower would be forgiven
If it disdained its brother;
And the sunlight clasps the earth
And the moonbeams kiss the sea:
What is all this sweet work worth
If thou kiss not me?

Percy Bysshe Shelley

If he loved with all the powers of his puny being, he couldn't love as much in eighty years as I could in a day.

Emily Brontë, Wuthering Heights

At first I only thought of being happy in you, – in your happiness: now I most think of you in the dark hours that must come – I shall grow old with you, and die with you – as far as I can look into the night I see the light with me. And surely with that provision of comfort one should turn with fresh joy and renewed sense of security to the sunny middle of the day. I am in the full sunshine now; and after, all seems cared for, – is it too homely an illustration if I say the day's visit is not crossed by uncertainties as to the return through the wild country at nightfall? – Now Keats speaks of 'Beauty, that must die – and Joy whose hand is ever at his lips, bidding farewell!' And who spoke of – looking up into the eyes and asking 'And how long will you love us'? – There is a Beauty that will not die, a Joy that bids no farewell, dear dearest eyes that will love for ever!

Robert Browning to Elizabeth Barrett Browning,
1846

Oh, No – Not Ev'n When We First Lov'd

Oh, no – not ev'n when first we lov'd
Wert thou as dear as now thou art;
Thy beauty then my sense mov'd
But now thy virtues bind my heart.
What was but Passion's sigh before
Has since been turn'd to Reason's vow;
And, though I then might love thee more,
Trust me, I love thee better now.

Although my heart in earlier youth
Might kindle with more wild desire,
Believe me, it has gain'd in truth
Much more than it has lost in fire.
The flame now warms my inmost core
That then but sparkled o'er my brow
And though I seem'd to love thee more
Yet, oh, I love thee better now.

Thomas Moore

If you're interested in finding out more about our
books, follow us on Twitter: @skyhorsepub

www.skyhorsepublishing.com